3 Supermarket Management Practices: In the Changing Economic Environment

3.1.4 Working Capital...28
3.2 The External Sources of Finance........................28
3.2.1 Shares...28
3.2.2 Loans or an Overdraft..................................29
3.2.3 Higher Purchase..29
3.2.4 Venture Capital...30
3.3 Profit and Loss Account...................................30
3.4 Balance Sheet...31
3.5 Budget for Exercising Financial Control................32
3.6 Importance of Cost Control...............................33
3.7 Problems from Unmonitored Costs & Budget.........33
3.8 Financial State of the Organisations....................34
3.9 How Controlling Budget Improves the Business Performance.........................34
3.10 Specific Points to Improve Performance..............36
4.0 Impact of Government Policies on the Supermarkets....................................36
4.1 Impact of the Government Expenditure on the Supermarkets........................38
4.2 Implication of Government Policies.....................40
4.3 Impact of Changes in the Economic Environment...41
4.4 Impact of Fiscal and Monetary Policy...................43
4.5 Effect of Fiscal and Monetary Policies on Business Operation of Supermarkets...44
4.6 Elements of Fiscal and Monetary Policies..............45
4.7 Impact of International Factors..........................45
5.0 Impact of the Changes in the Global Business & Economic Environments.........47

References..49
About the Author..53
Also By Ghazi Mokammel Hossain & GM Publishers..54

1.0 Introduction

Supermarket business is now a popular business in most of the countries of the world. Every year there are lots of new supermarkets starting their business in the different parts of the universe. But managing the business in this changing economic environment is always difficult for the owners and top management. So they need to develop and implement effective management practice to operate the business smoothly.

The book explains the connection between economic environment and the supermarket's management practices. For this reason, the author has been conducted a research on the two popular supermarkets of UK namely Tesco and ASDA. These two shops are the most popular supermarkets in the UK and operating their business in the different parts of the world as well.

The management system of these two supermarket chain corporations and effect of economic environment in these two business organizations are nicely discussed in this book. The book presents how the companies are effectively sustain their management practices in this changing economic environment. The author also tries to analyze the economic condition of these two supermarket chain corporations and tries to use the theoretical concepts of economics and business in the practical sense. Thus, most of the major concepts and theories are discussed in this book based on the real life scenario.

Copyright © 2016 by GM Publishers

The copyright of this book is registered by GM Publishers. None can publish this book or part of it without the permission of the publisher or author. No part of this publication may be reproduced, stored in a retrieval system, or transmitted in any form or by any means, electronic, mechanical, photocopying, reading, or otherwise, without the permission of the publishers or author. If anyone copy, publish, print and plagiarized the book will be illegal offence in the eye of law and be punished.

All rights are reserved. Published by GM Publishers

Supermarket Management Practices
In the Changing Economic Environment

Author: Ghazi Mokammel Hossain

Designer: Ghazi Mokammel Hossain

Publications Format: Amazon Kindle E-Book format, Amazon Createspace Paper back format

Edition No: First Edition, November, 2016

Publication From: UK

Version: International Version

Published by: GM Publishers, associated with Amazon Kindle Direct Publishing & Createspace

ISBN-13: 978-1539863052
ISBN-10: 1539863050 (The book has been assigned a CreateSpace ISBN)

Email address: gmpublishers04@gmail.com

Table of Contents

1.0 Introduction..4

1.1 What is Economic Environment of Business..5

1.2 Features of Economic Environment...6

1.3 Basic Elements of Economic Enviroment...6

1.4 Major Elements of Economic Enviroment...8

1.5 Important Factors of Economic Environment..9

1.6 Importance of Economic Environment Assessment...9

1.7 Economic Integration..10

1.8 What is Management Practice..11

1.9 Features of Effective Management Practice..12

1.10 Buying Decision Process for Supermarket...13

2.0 Impact of Economic Environment in the Management Practices of Supermarket.14

2.1 Tesco...15

2.2 ASDA...15

2.3 Employment and Recruitment...16

2.4 Recruitment Process..18

2.5 Purpose of Employment Contract..19

2.6 Description of Job...20

2.7 Employability Skill..20

2.8 Personal Skill...22

2.9 Physical Resource Contribution to the Success of the Organisation..................23

2.10 Technological Resources..24

3.0 Management of Human Resources Improves the Performance........................24

3.1 The Internal Sources of Finance for Tesco & ASDA......................................26

3.1.1 Retained Profit..26

3.1.2 Fixed Assets...26

3.1.3 Current Assets..27

Some basic concepts and theories are discussed in the first part. It will clear the idea of the readers to understand the practical implementation of the concepts and theories.

1.1 What is Economic Environment of Business?

Business and economic environment are the very important factors for any business organization.

It is not only important for the growth of the business, but also an important factor for the organizational development (Duhigg, 2012). An organization can only create its business environment, but can't create its economic environment. Because the economic environment can only be created by the govt. of the country. The definition of the economic environment of the business is as follows:

Economic environment of business determines all economic aspects or surroundings that greatly influence the business. The environment can create positive or negative impact on the business decision making, management, profit generation, cost and business expansion processes.

It is true that, the economic environment of the business is the part of the business environment. But this environment is the major part of the entire business environment.

1.2 Features of Economic Environment

There are some major features of the economic environment of business:

- Analyzing the inflation rate of a country
- Measuring the rate of unemployment within the country
- Debt calculation
- Distributing the income
- Controlling the poverty
- Analyzing the labor and production costs
- Identifying the productivity of the country through GNI and GDP

1.3 Basic Elements of Economic Enviroment

There are some basic elements of eceonomic enviroment which play a vital role in the development of business:

Economic Condition: Economic condition detemines the financial condition of the businesss organization and the country as well. The condition changes through the influence of the local and global economy.

Economic System: Economic system is the method that helps to produce goods and services for the society.

Different types of economic system are seen in the different countries of the world. Manily four types of eceonmic systems are prevailed in this world:

Four Economic Systems

An economic system is the method used by a society to produce and distribute goods and services.

Traditional economies rely on habit, custom, or ritual to decide what to produce, how to produce it, and to whom to distribute it.

In a **centrally planned economy** the central government makes all decisions about the production and consumption of goods and services.

In a **market economy** economic decisions are made by individuals and are based on exchange, or trade.

Mixed economies are systems that combine tradition and the free market with limited government intervention.

Economic Policies & Legislations: Economic policies and legislations are developed by the govt. of a particular country. Following are some examples of the economic policies & legislation:
- Fiscal Policy
- Monitory policy
- Trade Policy

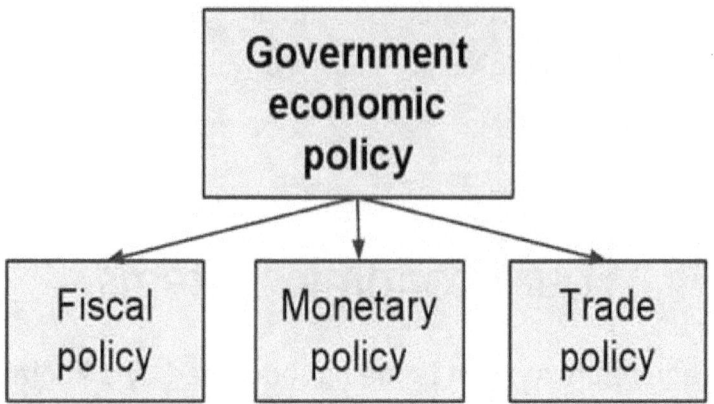

1.4 Major Elements of Economic Enviroment

There two major elements of eceonomic enviroment that influnce business:

- Gross National Income (GNI)
- Gross Domestic Product (GDP)

ELEMENTS OF ECONOMIC ENVIRONMENT

- **GROSS NATIONAL INCOME:**
  the income generated both by total domestic production as well as the international production activities of national companies.

  GROSS DOMESTIC PRODUCT:
  the total value of all final goods and services produced in a country in a given year equal to total consumer, investment, and government spending, plus the value of exports, minus the value of imports.

1.5 Important Factors of Economic Environment

Important factors of the economic environment are as follows:

Structure and nature of economy	Economic conditions	Economic policies	Global linkage
• Levels of development of the economy. • Sectoral composition of output. • Inter–sectoral linkage.	• Income levels. • Distribution of income. • GDP Trends. • Demand and supply trends. • Price trends. • Trade and BPO trends.	1. Industrial policy. 2. Trade policy. 3. Foreign exchange policy. 4. Foreign investment and technology policy. 5. Fiscal policy. 6. Monetary Policy.	• Magnitude and nature of cross border. • Trade flows. • Financial flows. • Membership of WTO, IMF, World Bank, trade blocs etc

1.6 Importance of Economic Environment Assessment

The importance of economic environment assessment is as follows:

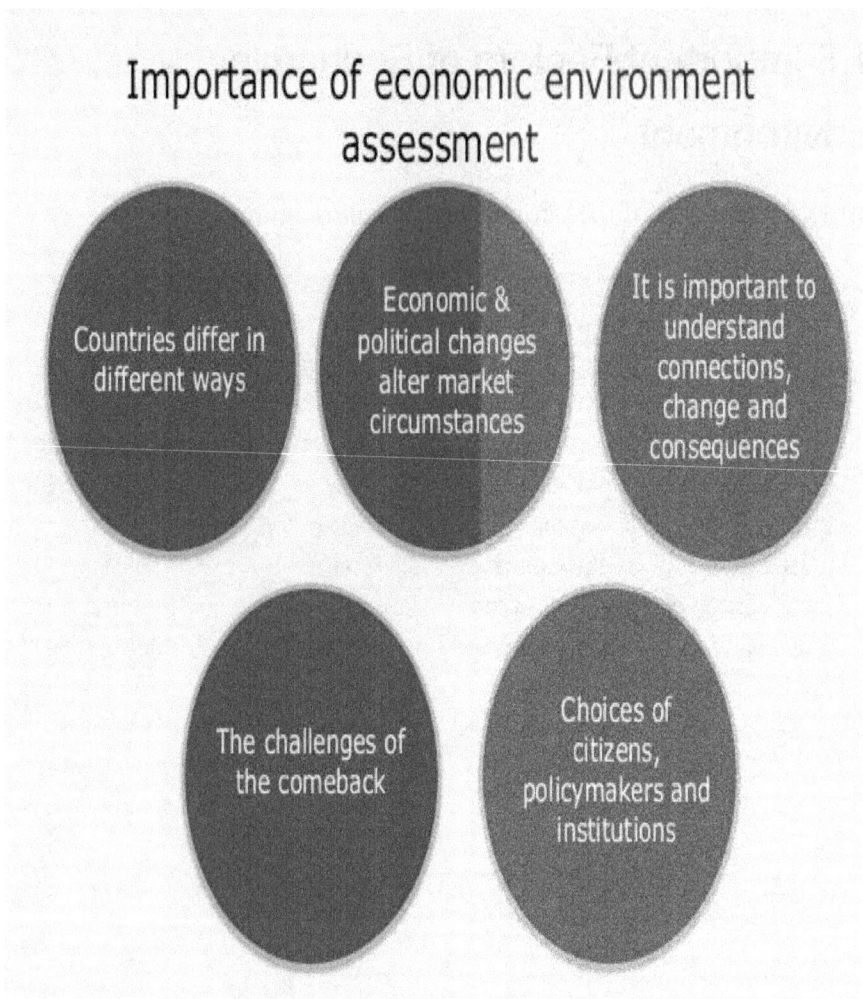

1.7 Economic Integration

Economic environment of business is integrated with some different economic entities this generally defines as economic integration. There are some forms of economic integration, these are given below

1.8 What is Management Practice?

Management practice is the business strategy of the organization, the practice helps an organization to achieve the goals with the help of all the departments of the organization.

Effective management practice is always necessary for every organization. In this context, the manager of the organization can play a vital role to control and monitor the management of the organization.

The top management of the organization develops this management practice but the manager of the organization is responsible to effectively monitor all the aspects of the practice

1.9 Features of Effective Management Practice

There are some important features of effective management practice:

- To deal with the changing economic environment
- To manage the employee in a professional way
- To create a strong leadership within the organization
- To create a friendly relationship between the employee and top management
- To achieve the goal of the organization quickly
- To create job oriented environment within the organization

1.10 Category Management Business Process for Supermarket

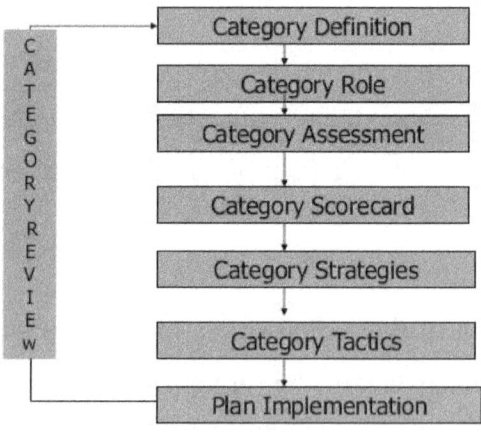

Supermarkets should implement the above category management process to establish their business strongly.

1.10 Buying Decision Process for Supermarket

As the economic environment of the business is gradually changing so the supermarkets should be familiar with this change. They should implement the following buying decision process to purchase products from the manufactures:

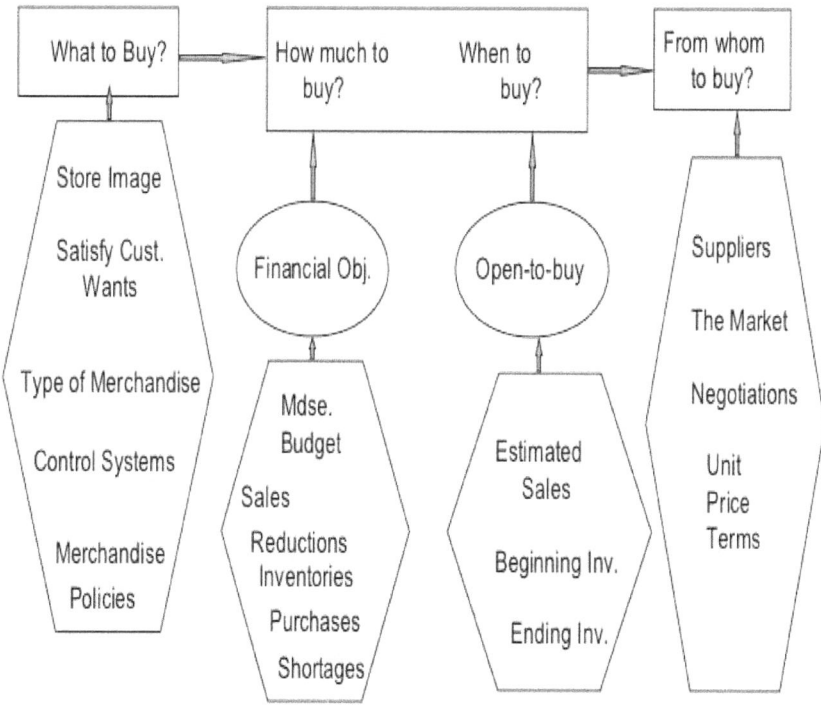

2.0 Impact of Economic Environment in the Management Practices of Supermarket

In this part, the author presents impact of economic environment in the real life scenario. The impact of economic environment has been discussed in the context of the two supermarket chain corporations such as ASDA and Tesco.

There are lots of supermarkets are available in the UK, namely Tesco, ASDA, Sainsbury's, Morrison, Waitrose etc. From those, ASDA is the largest supermarket and most resourceful supermarket chain corporation in the UK and global market (www.asda.com, 2016). As Tesco is also the largest chain supermarket in the UK, but they can't create a good position in the global market.

So this analysis will focus on the management, business and economic environments in the supermarket's business point of view. It will also analyze the Tesco and ASDA's economic and business environment. And how the organization is affected by the economic, govt., fiscal, monetary, international, etc. uprising factors. Finally the analysis will show all the reviews, all of the information and activities it has covered so far. And evaluate a result in the light of the impact of international factors.

2.1 Tesco

Introduction to Business Operation

Tesco is the UK's largest and most resourceful supermarket chain corporation on a global market. Tesco is an international brand, which can be easily understood by its expansion on the global platform. The organisation extended its operation into 12 countries including India, China, Malaysia, Czech Republic, Ireland, Poland and Hungary.

The core values mainly involve improvement in customer loyalty and develop excellent shopping experience. The organisation has always tried to establish a higher standard of goals in the existing competitive market. The corporation continuously adapts their business practices and strategies according to the global environment, setting a clear vision to a success of the organisation.

2.2 ASDA

Introduction to Business Operation

ASDA is acquired by Walmart in 1999, operating its business throughout the UK and the global business of the organization is maintained by parent organization Walmart (Corporate.walmart.com, 2015). Due to this ASDA has also been achieved a strong position in the local and global market as well.

As of August, 2016 ASDA has been managed second position in the UK's super market ranking table (Armstrong, 2016). Although Tesco has been achieved the first position, ASDA is trying hard to conquer the first position in the competitive UK's supermarket business. But the various economic and govt. related factors are creating problems to achieve this major goal (Armstrong, 2015).

The business organization is continuously affected by the slowdown exposed to the UK's food market. Besides, other external environments like, social, political, govt., technological, environmental and legislative, etc. also affecting the growth of the organization.

It is remarkable that, the changes in the rate of taxation or any other aspects can affect the financial condition of the organization (Kotler and Armstrong, 2012). For this reason, the organization is always changing their business policies to deal with the current external as well as internal environment.

2.3 Employment and Recruitment

Tesco and ASDA offers a wide range of job opportunities in their business operation. The organisations have divisions in their stores, which generate a wide scope of job opportunities for different candidates. The organisations always ensure that their working members work with an outstanding customer service and responsibility toward the organisation and the customers. The employment is structured according to the store and non-store jobs.

The store based jobs are mainly dealing with supervisors, check out employees, stock handlers and specialists like bakers and pharmacists. In the distribution sections, skilled workers manage stocks and logistics. Apart from these employments corporate offices requires a skilled person to manage the overall business process. The organisation has a simplified the way to reach the recruitment process (Holtbrügge and Ambrosius, 2015).

The applicant can filter their job requirement on the job portal according to category, role, location and keywords.

Apart from uncomplicated job sign up, the organisations also offer career advice for the better future. Recruitment is an essential element of workforce planning of the organisations, which allows the corporation to analyze the needs of employees in term of location, skill and number. The organisations are continuously extending their business operation, therefore job options are created for both food and non-food division of the business.

Tesco and ASDA have been divided their recruitment process into internal and external recruitment. Internal recruitment is based on the internal talent process to fill up the job option. For external recruitment process, the organisation advertises vacancies through their website, Facebook page, notifications on their stores, television, and radio or through advertisement on Google.

2.4 Recruitment Process

The recruitment process is an essential element in workforce planning, which involves recruiting a suitable candidate from the applications while maintaining the employment laws and regulations. Screening of the applicants plays a key role in selecting best candidate to be fit with the job requirement. Therefore, it is necessary for a selection procedure to filter the right candidate for a specific job in the organisation.

The screening round of these sorts of companies are mainly involved summarization of the CVs of the applicants whether the candidate matches the job specifications.

The procedure includes several stages to choose external management candidates (STAFSUDD, 2003). The next barrier is held by Assessment center controlled by the managers in the workplace, where the candidates are given different activities and problems solving exercises. After approval from the internal assessment process, the candidates have to face an interview procedure which ensures the eligibility of the candidate best suited for the vacant job option.

Through the recruitment and selection process of these companies, the organisations ensure effective and efficient candidates for their growth and development.

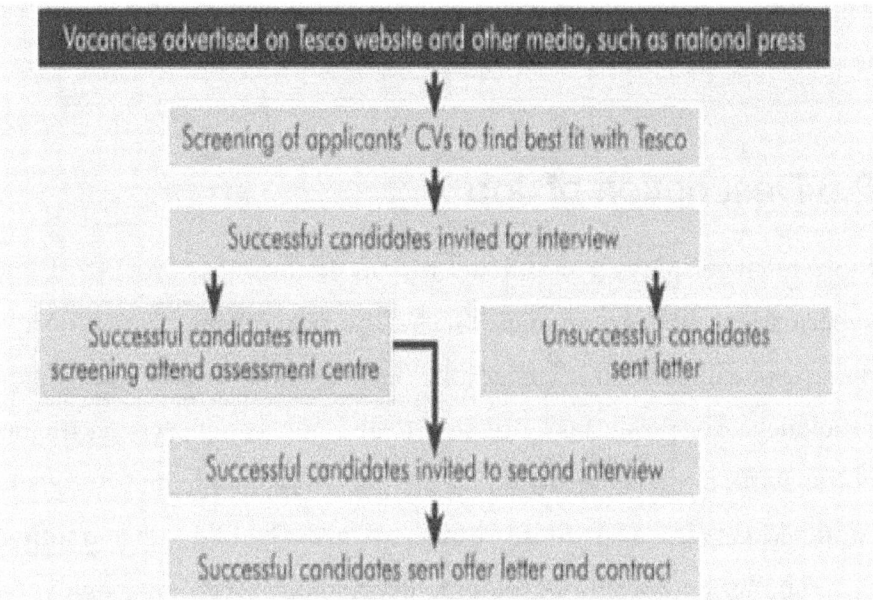

Figure: Recruitment Process of Tesco

2.5 Purpose of Employment Contract

The employment contract can be defined as the agreement between the organisation and employee, which governs their respective rights, obligations, duties and obligations. Employment contact helps in establishing a successful relationship between both the parties. Therefore, it is an essential element in a business operation, which secures the position of the organisation and the employees under certain rules and regulations.

The content of the employment contract depends on the job offered by an organisation, which mainly involves human rights and obligations in the workplace such as a safe workplace, notice period tenure, duty to obey and lawful orders (Yeung, 2011).

This process is very helpful for both the employer and the employee to avoid any disputes and ambiguity in business operation.

2.6 Description of Job

Store manager plays a significant role in the business process of the supermarkets like Tesco and ASDA. The position has the authority and responsibility to manage the entire store at the maximum efficiency. The basic task oriented to this job is supervision of the entire staffs in the store including the person in charge and Assistant Store Manager. The Store Manager also handles the training programmes and design development scheme for the new employees and existing staffs.

Apart from this, the position is responsible for variety internal operations like performance evaluation, personal actions, scheduling and payroll. Store Manager also delegates security measures, cash control, accounting system, in-stock maintenance and proper sanitation standards. Employability and personal skills are the essential elements to attain this position and for the future prospect (Jackson, 2013).

2.7 Employability Skill

The employment skill can be defined as the set of skill required for a specific job in an organisation. There are basically eight skills involved in the criteria, they are as follows

- ➢ **Communication:** Active questioning, listening and respond ensures positive store values.

- ➢ **Teamwork:** Active participation, collaboratively working with team members, supporting and understanding others are the essential aspects of a successful store management.

- ➢ **Problem-solving:** Anticipating problems and demonstrate sensibly is part of employability skill

- ➢ **Initiative and enterprise:** Adaptation to the changes and looking for positive aspects for the betterment of the store.

- ➢ **Planning and organising:** Understanding personal job role and planning task to avoid any uncertainties.

- ➢ **Self-management:** Includes understanding and following store policies by performing an inclusive behaviour.

- ➢ **Learning:** Includes personal strengths and weaknesses in context of the position.

- ➢ **Technology:** Knowledge about the available equipment and technology in the store.

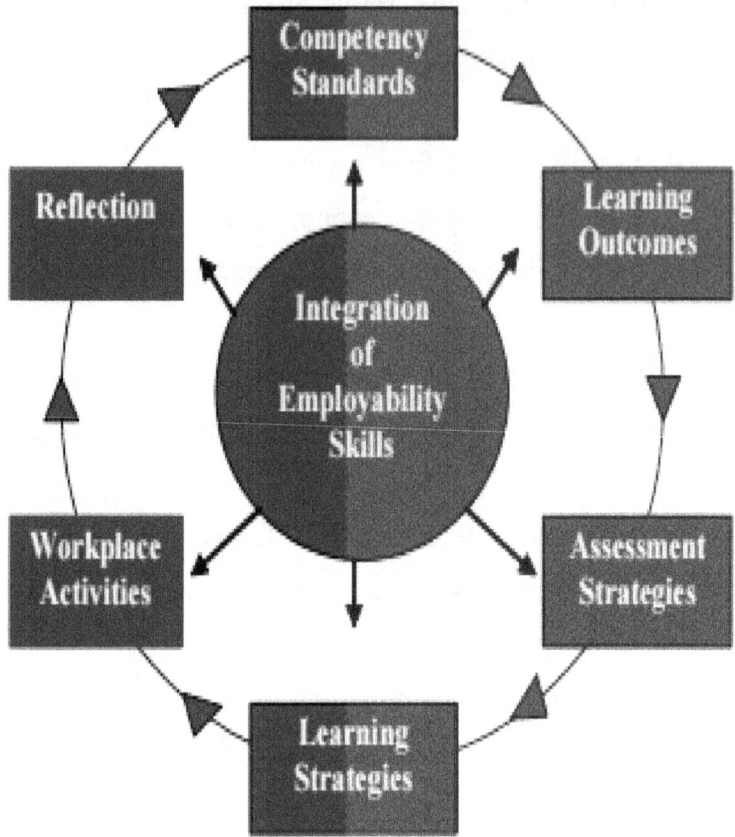

Figure: Integration of Employability Skill

2.8 Personal Skill

- ➢ Sincere and trustworthy are the essential personal attributes.
- ➢ Respectful to the organisation and other working employees.
- ➢ Cultural knowledge and sensitivity are significant.
- ➢ Flexibility and ethical in working place are necessary personal attributes.

2.9 Physical Resource Contribution to the Success of the Organisation

The physical resources of an organisation can be termed as the resources available to the business operation in the form of building, equipment, land and vehicles that are significant to the daily operation of the organisation. The effective management of physical resources is necessary for the successful operation of an organisation. The adaptive business strategy of Tesco and ASDA require supportive and adequate physical resources to extend their operation all over the world.

Tesco and ASDA have variety of business needs according to the location, size and environment. Therefore, lack of proper equipment and management process leads to unstable business operation. The physical resources of these companies are mainly categorized into six elements, they are building premises, equipment, plant, machinery, materials and stock. The equipment hardware equipment is maintained and managed carefully. The companies have a complex system of security measures, which includes CCTV, fire equipment, fire alarm system, security alarm and escapes.

The organisations have many features for excellent shopping experience for their customer. Online shopping is the unique feature of the organisations. Therefore, it is very important for any super store to manage and develop their physical resources to the overall development process of an organisation.

2.10 Technological Resources

Technological Resources are the elementary aspects of the modern business operations. The technological aspects are intangible elements managed in a similar manner as the physical resources of an organisation. The resources are mainly software, text and music, which is classified into four components they are as follows.

- Software Licensing
- Intellectual Property
- Accumulated Experience
- Patent and copyright

3.0 Management of Human Resources Improves the Performance

To enhance the process of business operation and to increase the performance of an organisation. It is necessary to manage the three kind resources effectively in a balanced form. The Human, Physical and Technological resources are the integral elements of an organisation.

Tesco has an excellent system managing capability of their resources and provide a benchmark for other organisation. ASDA has a huge potential to manage their employees in a professional manner which enhance the quality of their product and services (Alshibly, 2014).

The constructive approach of the management system leads to a positive attitude and helps the employee to work effectively in the workplace.

This process of management also involves a variety of development programmes, such as personal development planning, motivation, appraisal and training. The human resource management plays a vital role in achieving the goals and objectives of the organisation. Therefore, human resource management establishes a valuable bridge between the employees and the organisation (Gashi, 2013).

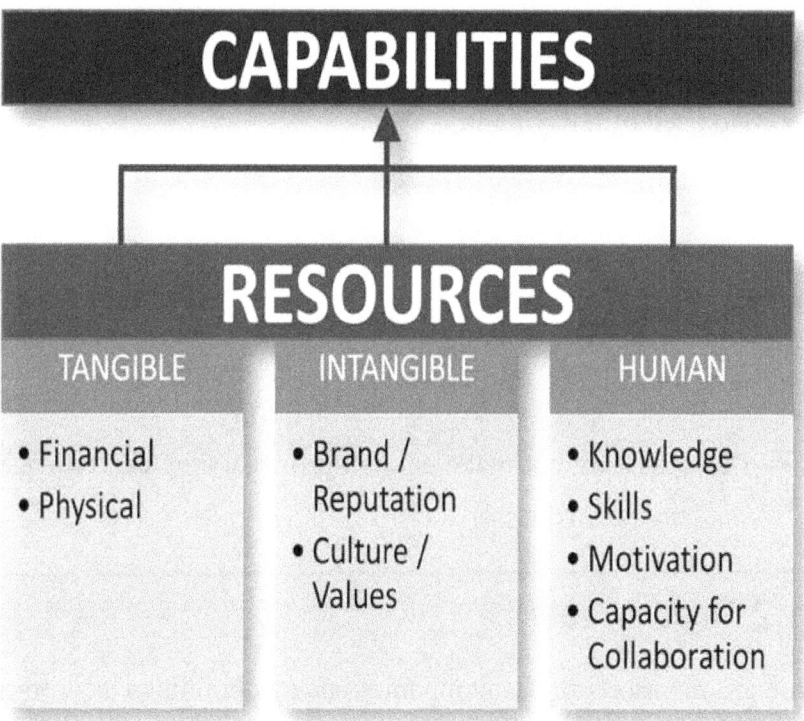

Figure: Resource Management Process of the Supermarkets

3.1 The Internal Sources of Finance for Tesco & ASDA

3.1.1 Retained Profit

This is the profit already made by the company which they can reinvest at the end of the year back into the company to improve the business on the basis of profit they made each year.

As Tesco and ASDA are the bigger organizations which make lots of profit per year, so they can reinvest the profit into their business.

Advantage

- No need of repaying it.
- Interest is not payable.

Disadvantage

- It is not available for new business
- Business may not make enough profit so they can reinvest it back to the business.

3.1.2 Fixed Assets

These are the assets of the companies such as buildings, equipment, vehicles etc. which they can use for funding future operations. These are the medium-term internal source of finance.

Advantage

- Finance can be raised from the assets which are no longer required.

Disadvantage

- Very slow method of raising funds
- Businesses have surplus assets to sell.

3.1.3 Current Assets

Current assets are one of the important internal sources for the company as they can be converted into cash easily. Company's stock is their current assets as they are transferred into cash after they are sold. It is a short-term source of internal finance. Current assets can be the key source of finance of the companies like Tesco, ASDA etc. as the companies can sell their stocks to retain their earnings and also the cash is converted easily.

Advantage

- Quick way for raising finance
- With selling the stock, the cost associated with holding them can be reduced.

Disadvantage

- Stock price reduced.

3.1.4 Working Capital

Working capital is the amount reserved for daily expenses.

Advantage

- Borrowed amount is reduced by the process like cutting stocks, delaying payments or chasing up the customers (Sun, 2015).

Disadvantage

- The solution is for very short time.

3.2 The External Sources of Finance

3.2.1 Shares

Tesco or ASDA can sell their shares to the new or existing shareholders for getting revenues from their investment.

Advantage

- Interest is not payable
- No need of repaying it.

Disadvantage

- Profits are paid to a number of shareholders.
- Company's ownership could change hands.

3.2.2 Loans or an Overdraft

ASDA or Tesco can borrow loans or an overdraft from the bank as an external source of finance. Bank provides loan on an interest rate either fixed or variable with a deposit. Overdraft is the short term loan with much higher rates of interest (Botez, 2012).

Advantage

- Loans are given for a set period of time, which is good for budgeting.
- If overdrafts are used for a short time then it is cheaper than the bank loan.

Disadvantage

- Loans can be expensive because of interest payment.
- The companies have to provide security for the loan.
- Overdrafts can be expensive if used for long period of time.

3.2.3 Higher Purchase

Higher purchase can help the supermarkets to acquire assets without buying it for full price. They can use it for vehicles, printers and machinery.

Advantage

- After all payments, the company can owe the assets.

- Businesses can use up to date equipment.

Disadvantage

- The costly method compares to another source of finance.

3.2.4 Venture Capital

This external source of finance is used mainly in the beginning of a new business.

Advantage

- Bring new experiences and knowledge.

Disadvantage

- Venture capital may bring huge returns, but it includes the high risk of failure.

3.3 Profit and Loss Account

Profit and loss of a financial statement mainly include the revenue, expenses and costs incurred during a fiscal quarter or a year. The profit and loss account provides data and information about the ability of the organisation to generate profit by reducing cost in business operation.

The statement provides net profit or net loss eliminating all income expenditure during the financial year.

Net profit can be observed when the total expenditure of the business is less than the sales and vice-versa. The profit and loss account produces an overview of the business, whether it will succeed or fail (Marginean, Mihaltan and Todea, 2015).

$$Revenue - Cost = Profit$$

3.4 Balance Sheet

The balance sheet is an essential element of the financial statement which includes a measurement analysis of the performance of the business operation. The element gives an overview of the whole debt and asset of the company, which is equivalent to the value of the company. The balance contains short-term and long-term debts, stock values, and capital assets, a value of shareholders' funds, reserves and debt to equity.

$$Capital + Liabilities = Assets$$

Analysis of economic environment of Tesco concludes strengths and weaknesses from the financial and non-financial aspects. The gross profit margin of the organisation is lower than the industries in average (Marilena and Alice, 2012).

This results in the financial weaknesses as the competitors like ASDA can gain higher gross profit. The operating profit margin is lower than average resulting Tesco at a better operational performance.

The priory of the organisation is to evaluate and cultivate the financial analysis in order to find out the weak or lacking areas in business operation. Therefore, an overall analysis of the balance sheet and income statement by different analytical tools and techniques are necessary for a successful business operation.

As ASDA is one of the top business organizations of UK, hence it also faces these kinds of issues. The environmental and political factors, issues of the UK and EU nations' govt. are effecting the working and performance level of the ASDA (www.asda.com, 2016).

3.5 Budget for Exercising Financial Control

The purpose of budgeting includes the forecast of income and expenditure, for decision making and to monitor business performance. Tesco and ASDA's budgeting are the essential parts of the business planning process. Budgeting helps ASDA and Tesco to provide a representation of how new business strategies, plans, events will work.

The purpose of budgeting in these companies are to measure the actual business performance with the forecast business performance. It will help the companies to know whether the business is matching the expectations.

3.6 Importance of Cost Control

For running the business of Tesco or ASDA in profit and to become more competitive, cost control is very important. The cost in a business is very vital. The cost in a business should be maintained so that it cannot exceed the budget prepared for the business.

If the cost becomes more than the budget prepared for the business then the business will face negative balance and the business will not make any profit (Viladàs, 2011). For bigger businesses such as ASDA, Tesco, if it face such a financial situation it will be difficult for them to take loans from the bank for doing future businesses. So cost control is essential. They can increase profits, preserve company's resources and improve productivity by the cost control

3.7 Problems from Unmonitored Costs & Budget

Supermarkets like ASDA and Tesco should monitor their cost and budget. If cost and budget are not monitored properly, then it is difficult to understand the performance of the company.

Unmonitored cost and budget lead to overspend and can go into debt. Without monitoring the cost and budget, the companies cannot find out the profit and loss in the market and also can't make the comparison with the competitors whether they are working better than them. Tesco can face unexpected situations if they failed to monitor their cost and budget. Same types of issue can be occurred in ASDA as well.

3.8 Financial State of the Organisations

Financial statement and analysis of Tesco, ASDA contain all the data regarding the financial condition of the organization for a period of time. These statements are the records of financial activities of Tesco/ASDA and provide an idea about the business financial condition.

Financial ratio analysis of Tesco is done for knowing the risk associated to the liquidity. Liquidity ratio consists of current ratio, financial leverage, debt equity ratio and quick ratio. Current ratio helps Tesco to know their liquidity aspect. It signifies whether Tesco is meeting the current obligation with its current assets. Same types of financial analysis is also seen in ASDA.

3.9 How Controlling Budget Improves the Business Performance

There are three steps in the determining and detailing a company in the achievement of a long-term goal, these are budgeting, planning and forecasting. The controller of the finance department manages this process.

Budgeting is a process where the overall plan which is executed on a monthly basis or daily basis. In addition, planning determines the outline of the company's financial direction and expectation for the future. Forecasting determines the accumulated past information to calculate financial outcomes for future years. This process in financial management helps in creating an outline which provide effective decision making by establishing the strategies, achieving the goal and objectives (Worthington and Britton, 2006).

Therefore, proper business planning ensures the awareness about the decision making for future aspect. The organisations like ASDA and Tesco have a successful businesses investment time to generate and control budgets, arrange and re-evaluate business plans and regularly supervise investment and performance. The structured planning of the supermarkets can make all the divergence to the development of food industries.

This causes in enabling the concentric capital on increasing the profits, dropping costs of production and growing returns on investment.

The planning prospect of the organisations help to reduce the complexity of financial work and business time. The most significant aspect of this process is that strategies are implemented and these causes in results are dynamic.

3.10 Specific Points to Improve Performance

Tesco and ASDA can increase their performance by improving the quality of the product and effective costs. In the supermarket industry, customers can easily shift from one store to another, so it is very important for Tesco/ASDA to retain their customers.

So, by offering a good quality product with reasonable prices the companies can attract and retain a number of customers. These companies can excel their growth in global retail stores and also can expand their business in online stores.

Tesco can improve their non-food sector by offering more variety to the customers. In this context, ASDA can store diversified category's product at their shops, this will help them to attract more customer to buy various types of product from their stores

4.0 Impact of Government Policies on the Supermarkets

Govt. is the supreme policy maker of any country or nation (Duhigg, 2012). Govt. develops policies for the wellbeing of a country. Govt. formulates policies for the development of social, political, economic, technological, legal, environment, business, and etc. environmental factors of the country. Sometimes, these policies can be stand as a harmful factor in the economic development of the country (Gani and Clemes, 2013).

These harmful issues can badly affect the business organizations of the country. UK is one of the top most developed countries in the world. It's not only a developed country, but also has a strong democratic political environment (Gani and Clemes, 2013). But some govt. policies of the nation now badly affecting the business organizations of the country.

According to the UK's and EU nations' policy, the business organization located in these nations have to recruit local or native work force for the different position of the business organization (Gillanders and Whelan, 2014). This policy is now greatly affecting the business and economic environment of the ASDA and Tesco. Because the salary or the price range of the local work force is quite high than the Asian or African workforce. As the companies try to merge its business locally and globally, thus this policy has created a barrier to reach their goals (Corporate.walmart.com, 2015).

According to the rule of UK's and EU nations' govt. the companies who're operating their business in this continent, are unable to take advance payment for the order of the products and other kinds of activities from the suppliers (Griffin and Ebert, 2004). As ASDA, Tesco have been operating their business in this continent from the long time period, so they are also facing this burning rule (www.asda.com, 2016). The govt. of UK strongly monitors the price of the goods and services of the supermarkets, hence Tesco and ASDA always try to reduce their products or services price range.

4.1 Impact of the Government Expenditure on the Supermarkets

Govt. of a country spends the money for the development of the nation. This expenditure has been done for the development of public, private, charitable, environment, business, economic and other sectors. It also helps the govt. to promote high living standards for the people of the country (Gillanders and Whelan, 2014). The govt. of a country develops some strong taxation policies in order to compensate with the high expenditure.

The govt. of UK imposes high taxation and interest rate for the private or the public sector's organizations. The companies like Tesco and ASDA are also facing the negative impacts of the policies and stopped their marginalization process due to high tax and interest rate (www.asda.com, 2016).

The govt. of UK has imposed National Insurance Tax (NI Tax) and Value Added Tax (VAT) for the local as well as the foreign business organizations (Griffin and Ebert, 2004). The goal of this taxation strategy is to cope with the expenditure of the govt. but these VAT and NI tax policies increase the expenditure of the business organization like ASDA and Tesco.

For these high taxation and insurance policies, ASDA has been reduced their selling departments, even stopped some of their local stores in the different parts of the UK (Griffin and Ebert, 2004). They even failed to cope with the market competition and once secured third position in the UK's supermarket ranking table (www.asda.com, 2016). Tesco also cuts up their development budget to deal with this circumstance.

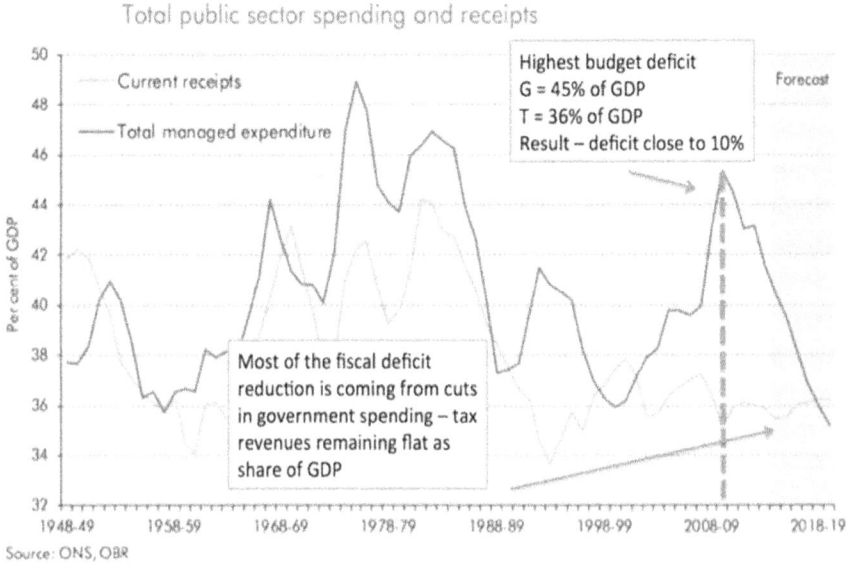

Figure: Govt. Expenditure and Taxation in UK

But now they are formulating some new strategies to recover from this breakdown. One of the finest strategies of these companies are their high standard promotional strategy, the companies spend more money on the promotional activities in order to compensate.

Because a large number of promotional activities can take more customers to their supermarkets, this strategy can also help the organizations in order to compensate with the rules and policies of the govt. (Klapper and Love, 2014). In this way, govt. expenditure meets up policies have both positive as well as negative roles in the business process of supermarkets

4.2 Implication of Government Policies

The business process of ASDA and Tesco are greatly influenced by the positive and negative policies of the govt. As the supermarkets operate their business throughout the UK and EU countries, so they have to maintain these rules in order to run their business legally (Corporate.walmart.com, 2015).

The govt. provides various types of services for the business organizations like, free training opportunities for the workforce of the particular organization, loan facilities for the business organization, etc. Both ASD and Tesco can take these opportunities that can help them to rise their business eventually.

Besides, govt. also provides direct or indirect support for the weaker business organizations who're taking a loan from the govt. to rise or develop their business. It includes, reduced taxation policy linked with VAT, corporation tax and NI taxes. The supermarkets can also take this advantage, it will help the organization to reduce the expenditure and develop their business gradually. The govt. of UK provides infrastructure for the development of new business, it also encourages the local as well as the foreign investors to invest in this country (Griffin and Ebert, 2004).

The govt. of UK imposes low amount of tax for those who're investing on the govt. provided land or infrastructure. Supermarkets like ASDA and Tesco should use the govt. infrastructure, by doing this they can reduce their costs and increase their net profit (Corporate.walmart.com, 2015).

4.3 Impact of Changes in the Economic Environment

The strong taxation and other economic policies of the UK as well as the EU govt. are greatly impacting the economic environment of the supermarkets like ASDA or Tesco. Due to the unstable economic condition, due to the simultaneous economic recession from 2008 to 2013 in the UK and EU the business organizations are facing economic crisis (Gani and Clemes, 2013).

This also greatly impacts the economic environment of ASDA and other supermarket chain shops. During the period of recession, the customers are not intended to buy more products or services from these types of chain shops. So the supermarket chain corporation like ASDA, Tesco fall into economic crisis.

The high taxation rate also forces to increase the price of products, it adds some extra charges for every single product. Suppose, the price of a Book is 12 pounds, it can be converted to 14.22 pounds due to the 18.5% VAT imposed by the govt. So this excessive level of taxation policies can badly affect the economic environment of the supermarket chain shop business (Luo and Zhao, 2009). The fluctuation in the price of the products and services lower the probability of the customer to buy the commodity and service (Watts, 2007).

In 2016, UK govt. has been approved Brexit after the results of United Kingdom European Union membership referendum, 2016 goes in favour of this, 51.89% voters wanted to leave the EU this forced the govt. to approve the demand of public. But this is gradually declining the economic position of UK and various business organizations of the country suffer much. The price of the GBP is gradually falling and it can be touched the price of US dollar very soon.

Hence the company like ASD, Tesco have been fallen into deep economic crisis to maintain the profitability of the business. Not only these companies but the other companies of the different business sectors are also fallen in the same type of financial crisis. Some researches show that Brexit has been created a big issues in the development and profitability of the business organization. This also creates a crisis situation in the stable economy of UK.

Changes in economic environment can create various types of issues like formulation of new rules, regulations and policies by the govt. to cope with the gradual changes in the economy (Luo and Zhao, 2009). ASDA and Tesco are trying to cope with this unstable economic market. The business organizations are selling high quality products in their stores to attract a large number of customers to buy the quality products at a reasonable price (Corporate.walmart.com, 2015). This strategy is not only helping them to make a large number of loyal customer or consumer, but also helped them to increase the profit margin.

4.4 Impact of Fiscal and Monetary Policy

The business operations of the ASDA and Tesco are operated by the various types of Fiscal and Monetary Policies made by the govt. of UK. These policies are formulated by the parliament members of the govt. (Klapper and Love, 2014). The business operations of the supermarkets are greatly affected by these govt. policies, those are as follows:

Govt. Expenditure: The expenditure of the govt. directly affect the sales and revenue of the supermarkets. Due to the more expenditure in the public sectors by the govt., the sales of the Tesco and ASDA have been decreased. It can be increased if the govt. spend more money for the private sectors.

Exchange Rates: Exchange rates can play a major role in the development of the business organization like Tesco or ASDA. As the exchange rate of the GBP is declining day by day than the other currencies like Dollars and Euro, so the business organization are facing trouble to develop its business in local as well as the foreign lands (Klapper and Love, 2014).

Interest Rate: Interest rate is maintained by following the monetary policy of the govt. With the decreased interest rate, supermarket like ASDA, Tesco can increase its sales volume. Because decrease interest rate gives the customers a big opportunity to consume more products. But the increased interest rate will not promote the customers to consume more products, this will negatively impact on the Tesco and ASDA's sales volume level.

Tax Rates: Increased tax rate will increase the price of the products. So the business organizations like ASDA and Tesco increase their product price. But the decreased tax rates can reduce the price of the products of the companies. It can also promote the customers to buy a quality product at a cheap price.

4.5 Effect of Fiscal and Monetary Policies on Business Operation of Supermarkets

Fiscal and monetary policies are greatly affecting the operation of the supermarkets. These two policies are being formulated by the govt. to develop and control the economic conditions of a country (Pride, Hughes and Kapoor, 1999).

Fiscal policy is a method that can control and monitor the spending and tax rates of the govt. On the other hand, monetary policy is the sister strategy of the fiscal policy, by which the govt. of a country controls the money supply in the money market to reduce the rates of inflation or interest (Pride, Hughes and Kapoor, 1999). It also creates a price stability and general trust in the currency.

As the UK's govt. gradually spends more money in the different sectors like public, private, infrastructure, defenses, education, etc., hence it's increasing the taxation and interest rates. It will greatly impact the business operation of supermarkets. Govt. of UK is strongly controlling the money supply in the market to reduce the rate of inflation. They also control the high price of pound to stabilize the local along with international market (Gillanders and

Whelan, 2014). This can decrease the volume of sales as well as the net profit of the supermarkets like Tesco and ASDA.

4.6 Elements of Fiscal and Monetary Policies

The elements of fiscal and monetary policy help the business organizations to formulate new rules, regulations and business plan to maintain the growth of the business. The fiscal policy is made by the govt. and also regulated by the govt. (Pride, Hughes and Kapoor, 1999). And the monetary policy of the country is formulated by the govt. but controlled by the central bank of the country. As the rate of the VAT in UK is 20%, so it is the duty of the govt. to decrease the rate at 17.5%.

It will not increase the net profit of the business organizations but increase the annual revenue of the govt. It will assist ASDA and Tesco to provide better products to its customer by maintain the same price range. Besides, the central bank of the UK should maintain the same interest rate of 0.5%.

It will help ASDA, Tesco and other companies to add extra revenue in the govt. fund (Klapper and Love, 2014). This will also help the supermarkets to increase its business operations and provide quality services to the customer.

4.7 Impact of International Factors

There various types of international factors, those play a vital role in the business operations of the supermarkets while operating its business in the local and foreign market (www.asda.com, 2016). Those factors are discussed below:

Business Environment: The business environment of a country includes, economic, social, political, cultural, legal, technological etc. factors. As ASDA and Tesco operate its business globally, hence it's always trying hard to maintain these environments to run the business smoothly (www.asda.com, 2016).

Tax & VAT: ASDA and Tesco are the global business organizations, it face different tax and VAT rates in the different countries. UK and EU nations' tax, VAT etc. rates are not the same, so the supermarkets maintain different price structures for the different countries (www.asda.com, 2016).

International Competition: The supermarkets like Tesco and ASDA always face international competition while operating its business globally (www.asda.com, 2016). Because lots of global supermarket chain corporations are the main competitors of this business organization.

But ASDA is very nicely handling these competitors with the help of Walmart, while Tesco suffers much to operate its business in the international markets.

Exchange Rates: Tesco and ASDA's global business is greatly affected by the unstable exchange rates. ASDA and Tesco will face great challenges if the exchange rate of the UK falls down with that of other nations.

5.0 Impact of the Changes in the Global Business & Economic Environments

The global and European business, economic environments are gradually changing (Klapper and Love, 2014). Due to simultaneous recessions in the EU as well as international economy the business and economic environments are rapidly changing (Klapper and Love, 2014).

EU has developed some policies for those business organizations who're operating their businesses in the EU countries, some of them are given below:

- Employment policy
- Training and educational policy
- International policy
- Taxation policy
- Regional policy
- Inflation policy

The supermarket chain corporations like Tesco and ASAD are trying hard to deal with the changing business environment of the EU and the entire world.

The organization is trying to operate their business legally by maintaining all the policies of the EU and different nations (www.asda.com, 2016).

As the global retail and supermarket competitions are gradually increasing, hence these types of supermarkets should be more careful about business policy making.

It can assist the business organizations to rise its business in the global market.

References

Alshibly, H. (2014). Evaluating E-HRM success: A Validation of the Information Systems Success Model. *ijhrs*, 4(3), p.107.

Armstrong, A. (2015). *Asda snatches back title of UK's second largest supermarket*. [online] Telegraph.co.uk. Available at: http://www.telegraph.co.uk/finance/newsbysector/retailandconsumer/11822351/Asda-snatches-back-title-of-UKs-second-largest-supermarket.html [Accessed 14 Dec. 2015].

Botez, D. (2012). Internal Audit and Management Entity. *Procedia Economics and Finance*, 3, pp.1156-1160.

Corporate.walmart.com, (2015). *Walmart Locations Around the World - United Kingdom*. [online] Available at: http://corporate.walmart.com/our-story/locations/united-kingdom#/united-kingdom [Accessed 14 Dec. 2015].

Duhigg, C. (2012). *The power of habit*. New York: Random House.

Gashi, R. (2013). Strategic Human Resources Management: Human Resources or Human Capital. *AJIS*.

Gani, A. and Clemes, M. (2013). Modeling the effect of the domestic business environment on services trade. *Economic Modelling*, 35, pp.297-304.

Gillanders, R. and Whelan, K. (2014). Open For Business? Institutions, Business Environment and Economic Development. *Kyklos*, 67(4), pp.535-558.

Griffin, R. and Ebert, R. (2004). *Business*. Upper Saddle River, NJ: Prentice Hall.

Holtbrügge, D. and Ambrosius, J. (2015). Mentoring, skill development, and career success of foreign expatriates. *Human Resource Development International*, 18(3), pp.278-294.

Jackson, D. (2013). Employability skill development in work-integrated learning: Barriers and best practice. *Studies in Higher Education*, 40(2), pp.350-367.

Klapper, L. and Love, I. (2014). The Impact of Business Environment Reforms on New Registrations of Limited Liability Companies. *The World Bank Economic Review*.

Kotler, Philip, and Gary Armstrong. *Principles of Marketing*. Boston: Pearson Prentice Hall, 2012. Print.

Luo, Y. and Zhao, H. (2009). Doing Business in a Transitional Society: Economic Environment and Relational Political Strategy for Multinationals. *Business & Society*, 52(3), pp.515-549.

Marginean, R., Mihaltan, D. and Todea, N. (2015). Structure Ratios of Profit and Loss Account – Source of Information for Performance Analysis. *Procedia Economics and Finance*, 26, pp.396-403.

Marilena, Z. and Alice, T. (2012). The Profit and Loss Account– Major Tool for the Analysis of the Company's Performance. *Procedia - Social and Behavioral Sciences*, 62, pp.382-387.

Pride, W., Hughes, R. and Kapoor, J. (1999). *Business*. Boston: Houghton Mifflin Co.

STAFSUDD, A. (2003). RECRUITMENT POLICY VS. RECRUITMENT PROCESS: ESPOUSED THEORY AND THEORY-IN-USE. *Academy of Management Proceedings*, 2003(1), pp.G1-G6.

Sun, Y. (2015). Internal Control Weakness Disclosure and Firm Investment. *Journal of Accounting, Auditing & Finance*.

Viladàs, X. (2011). Measuring Design's Contribution to Business Success: A Three-Tier Approach.*Design Management Review*, 22(2), pp.54-60.

Worthington, I. and Britton, C. (2006). *The business environment*. Harlow: Financial Times Prentice Hall.

Watts, D. (2007). A glossary of UK government and politics. Edinburgh: Edinburgh University Press.

www.asda.com, (2016). *Asda.com - Online Food Shopping, George, & more*. [online] Available at: http://www.asda.com/ [Accessed 14 Sept. 2016].

Yeung, R. (2011). *Successful interviewing and recruitment*. London: Kogan Page.

About the Author

Ghazi Mokammel Hossain is a professional e-book, article, research, analysis paper and a creative writer. He has written some books as well as many articles, research papers, analysis and creative articles. The author is also a freelance writer as well as a researcher. He was born on 31 December, 1993. He has passed his S.S.C exam from Dhaka under Dhaka Board in 2008 and passed his H.S.C exam from Dhaka under Dhaka Board in 2010. He has graduated with a Bachelor's of Business Administration in HRM in 2015 from a renowned University. He has also completed Computer Science and Engineering certificate course in 2011.

He published his first book called "IPv4 IP6 Technology & Implementation" in Amazon Kindle and Createspace on 2013. The author published his second book called "Introduction to Network on Chip Routing Algorithms" in 2014. He also published "Fundamental of API Based Financial Engineering" and "Ebola Epidemic: A Detail Survival Guide From Ebola Virus Disease Outbreak" in 2014. The author published an outstanding thrilling novel called "Anwar: Emergence of Unknown Defenders" in 2016 on Amazon kindle and Createspace. Playing football, Cricket, PC games, reading books, novel, research paper, cycling and mountain climbing are his favorite hobbies.

Also By Ghazi Mokammel Hossain & GM Publishers

Supermarket Management Practices: In the Changing Economic Environment- November, 2016 by Ghazi Mokammel Hossain

Anwar: Emergence of Unknown Defenders- August 10, 2016 by Ghazi Mokammel Hossain
https://www.amazon.com/dp/B01K8KLIJ8

The Survival of USA – Part Two: A Novel - August, 2016 by Ghazi Mokammel Hossain & MD. Fazle Mubin
https://www.amazon.com/dp/B01K8I4Z0E

Business Environment: Theoretical & Organizational Aspects – July, 2016 by Ghazi Mokammel Hossain
https://www.amazon.com/dp/B01HTQYG7A

The Survival of USA - Part One: A Novel – March, 2016 by Ghazi Mokammel Hossain, MD. Fazle Mubin & Pranjal Rahman
https://www.amazon.com/dp/B01CTXNF8E

Enterprise IPv6 for Enterprise Networks- December, 2015 by Ghazi Mokammel Hossain & Fathe Mubin
https://www.amazon.com/dp/B017U84ISO

Heart of Democracy: A Versatile Poetry Book - Aug 28, 2015 by Ghazi Mozammel Hossain
https://www.amazon.com/dp/B014MTHGRY

The Brave Parrot of Jungle - Dec 11, 2014 by Syeda Taskin Ara & Gulshan Ahmed
https://www.amazon.com/dp/B00QXHW4PS

IPv4 IPv6 Technology and Implementation - Nov 2, 2013 by Ghazi Mokammel Hossain & GM Hossain

https://www.amazon.com/dp/B00GEHNC8K

The Mirror of Religion - Jul 19, 2015 by Ghazi Mozammel Hossain & Richard Marks

https://www.amazon.com/dp/B01204ROIO

Introduction to Network on Chip Routing Algorithms - Oct 4, 2014 by Ghazi Mokammel Hossain

https://www.amazon.com/dp/B00O6ET3J0

Ebola Epidemic: A Detail Survival Guide From Ebola Virus Disease Outbreak - Oct 25, 2014 by Ghazi Mokammel Hossain & Dr. Robert Alex

https://www.amazon.com/dp/B00OWG4TL4

Fundamental of API Based Financial Engineering - Oct 17, 2014 by Ghazi Mokammel Hossain

https://www.amazon.com/dp/B00OJJJJO6

For more details please visit Amazon Author Central

https://www.amazon.com/Ghazi-Mokammel-Hossain/e/B00GGATR2K/ref=dp_byline_cont_ebooks_1

GM Publishers

My Book My Life

www.ingramcontent.com/pod-product-compliance
Lightning Source LLC
Chambersburg PA
CBHW061223180526
45170CB00003B/1134